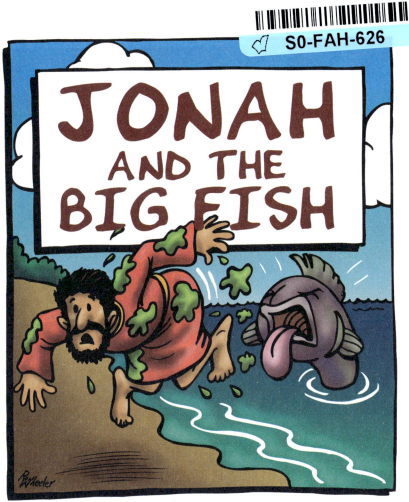

JONAH
AND THE
BIG FISH

By Mark Ammerman

Illustrations by Ron Wheeler

God said to Jonah, "Go to the city of Nineveh. Tell the people there that I am angry because of their terrible, awful sins! Warn them that they must change or I will destroy them."

But Jonah didn't want to warn the people of the city of Nineveh. So he disobeyed God. Instead of going to Nineveh, he got on a ship and sailed far away in the other direction.

But God sent a stormy wind onto the ocean. The wind made big waves crash against Jonah's ship. The ship started filling up with water!

The ship's sailors were very afraid. They even
threw things into the sea to help keep the ship
from sinking.

But Jonah was sound asleep in a room at the bottom of the ship. The ship's captain found him there.

"Why are you sleeping?" shouted the captain.
"Wake up, lazy man! Get up and call to your
God! Maybe He will save us!"

Then the sailors asked, "Which one of us has done an evil thing to cause the gods to be so angry?"

They decided it must be Jonah's fault. "What have you done?" the scared sailors asked him. "Who are you? Where are you from?"

And Jonah said sadly, "I am a Hebrew, and I fear the God of heaven who made the earth and the oceans."

Then he told the sailors, "God asked me to go to Nineveh. But I disobeyed Him and ran away on this ship." He sighed. "This storm is all my fault."

"Throw me off the ship into the water," said Jonah quietly. "Then God will calm the sea and you will be safe."

So they took Jonah up to the ship's deck and
threw him into the sea. And the wind stopped
blowing! And the sea grew calm.

Then God sent a great big, hungry fish to swallow Jonah. Jonah sat in the belly of that old fish for three days and three nights!

Jonah prayed. "Oh Lord, You threw me into the deep waters and I thought I was dead for sure! But then I remembered that You can still save me. Please save me, Lord!"

And God told the fish to spit Jonah out upon the dry land. Then God said, "Go to Nineveh and tell them what I told you to do in the first place."

So Jonah went. (Wouldn't you?) When he got to Nineveh, he shouted in the streets, "God will destroy Nineveh forty days from now unless you change the way you live!"

The king of Nineveh heard Jonah—and he believed him! He told all his people to stop sinning and to pray that God would forgive them.

When God saw that the people of Nineveh
stopped being bad, He decided not to destroy
their city after all. God is kind and good and
patient.

Then Jonah was mad at God. "I knew You would save them! So why did You make me come all the way here to tell them You wanted to destroy them?"